MIND'S UNCERTAIN VIBE

ANANYA BARUAH

I have never got to see my grandfather in my life. He passed away before I was born ,though his presence is always felt by us . I am extremely grateful to him . Atlast I offer my sincere gratiude to him .Please bless me from the heaven .

I wholeheartedly dedicate this book to him.

Your grandaughter Ananya Baruah

Late Shri Phatik Kumar Baruah

Contents

Preface

Though my prefernce of writing this book is not to earn fame,money or popularity .I want to record all my thoughts how my mind sends me uncertain thought and its solutions .I want to relate to people who are suffering sometimes they feel guilty on themselves . Well a disclaimer to all my readers ,I am not a topper nor an innate philosopher .I am just a simple girl who wants to breake the chain of Depression , Introvertness and self-doubting on yourself .During my childhood days I was not a bright student but deep inside I used to sense every aspect of bitterness and sweetness in my life .Well I can say that I was an innate empathy i.e I can understand other people's feeling and emotions even I can give them solutions but if they are sad because of their breakup .Sorry I can't help them with it. Anyway after a certain period I started finding the reality of life.At this age when we are growing we would often get some unnecesary thought though some useful ,you might start getting moodswings you have your own likes and dislikes .Then at this age you might have crushes which happens uncontrollably .But at that time we should not forget our responsibilities neglecting them will cause a big problem in the future . We might feel distracted from our path sometimes . This is not a serious issue it is due to biological reason i.e our brain releases some kinds of hormones which are responsible for changes in our feeling and emotion .Due to which we often spend our precious time on works which gives us pleasure for a short period of time as an outcome we feel regret and guilty and often it destroys our productivity . Our mind also plays a crucial role in taking decession . "DOPAMINE " an hormone which is responsible for providing us pleasure releases simultaneously upon doing any work which provides us pleasure instantly like frequently watching phone ,food craving etc.It destroys our thoughts ,creativity and productivity . Sometimes our mind becomes so disturbed that we feel motionless, legarthic and loss interest in our work and couldn't find a way to escape . But there is an universal truth every problem has an unique solution .Thus we shouldn't be scared of the turmoil in our lives . Instead we should fought against them bravely with courage and confidence .

Acknowledgements

I want to thank my parents who encouraged me to frame my thoughts and views in to a book. And special thanks to Notion press who made this possible and gave my book an appropriate platform to display.

ONE
ACHIEVING LITTLE STEPS

Ever wondered how a person becomes a great person well no one has achieved the pinnacle of the mountain at one move . Covering the steps subsequently made them reach their goal . From childhood my inspiration has been Mary Kom .I aspire to pursue Martial Arts after watching her movie . Whenever I face failure my mom would always encourage me by giving her as an example . She would tell me "look at Mary kom she reached the summit of Boxing because of her hardwork and workholic attitude ,she didn't let her poor background be an obstacle in her boxing career.Hearing this my energy level would boost up but as you know we are in psychological human life not in a Bollywood movie where a person can acheive sucess within a minute I would loose all those motivations which I gained. Always try to break the obstacles which are hampering your work .

Enter Caption

TWO
VIRTUAL WORLD

In today's world mobile phones have become an integral part of our social life . People often likes to share their day to day life in the internet . Well it seems a good mode of entertainment but when it becomes habitual we get intense doubt about ourself . Sometimes we start comparing our life with others we often mistook other's life to be perfect thus creating confussion and sadness .Obviously nowadays quitting social media is just as to avoid a slice of pizza . One of the reason we sometimes don't feel our life to be perfect is because we are surrounded by social media . Well it has it's own positive and negative sides . It sometimes provides informatic videos and sometimes it turns to misguide us . No matter problems are part of our life but we need to handle them calmly not harshly . No one can change the past but we can change our future with today's work and mindset .

Enter Caption

THREE
CONTROLLING EMOTIONS

At a time you will be so overwhelmed with your thoughts that you will be having unnecessary thought arising in your mind ,sometimes you might also feel guilty ,on yourself for your action or behaviour .I have seen some people who wants to change their character or behaviour like a character from a movie .For example being too cute ,too clumsy ...aego! Dear you don't have to change yourself for someone admire the person you are .Often we feel ashamed of the way we dress well don't be ashamed of your dressing sense .Your mind have various chains to break . If you want to avoid your bad habits just try to push yourself hard ,once you thought of changing the system don't look back know your value you are worth of everything .Just have a mindset if they can acheive it why not me . People have two personalities introvert and extrovert . Well Intovert people have their own superpowers .Introverts enjoy their own company .Outside they are silent and calm but deep inside they are mastermind .Extrovert person they are kind a darring person.

Enter Caption

d of daring person .

FOUR
MAKING FRIENDS

Friends are those who are connected to us without any blood relations .After our parents we feel more safe and secure with our friends with whom we can we share all our feeling . My parents have often adviced me to be friends with the one who is good in studies well they are but it not need to be proved that those students who are bad in their studies need to be a bad person . It depends on us whether we want to camouflage with them or be a stone who doesn't camouflage with its surrounding but our feelings and aspects of life should match with them . It doesn't mean sharing all our secrets some secrets needs to be within you don't disclose it outside .

In life we have only one choice where we can choose someone of our own where no one can intefere . We can't choose our parents neither we can choose our relatives but we can choose our friends . So choose your friend wisely . Whatever happens you are responsible for it.

Enter Caption

FIVE
STUDIES

The word study common to all right? with study you can acheive anything in the world even you can beat Elon Musk funny right? I know from the beginning only I was really worse in studies ,though I was good in other curricular activities like dancing ,singing and martial arts but why this happens so ? Some will say it is a skill that is developed in a child within it's birth .But according to me it is not so . You can't be pigeon hooked on the basis of your skill .You will find lots of motivational videos in youtube most probably "How to get good marks without studying " well I was among one of the viewers . I had tried lots of strategy within me one of them was thinking opposite ,In our lives ,we have faced the opposite of what we think . So I thought of applying this to my studies and timidly it worked but deep inside I was not satisfied then while scrolling youtube I came across a book named Atomic Habits . Everyone's review was superb , well I didn't purchased the book as I ended up having lots of book without completing them . So I read it in google .It is the best book for habit development but how is study related to habits ? So closely related .At the beginning I have mentioned you that I was good in music ,dance and martial arts But why? During the course of dance you will be taught basic steps ,body posture its orign . How much energy you have to apply ,schools also have level 1,2,3,4... learning ABCD.. 1,2,3,4... is the basis for knowledge ,naming sentence ,doing calculations .

Enter Caption

SIX

TECHNIQUES TO STUDY

It depends on us on what criteria we are studying . Some people study to get a job ,good salary but we should study for our own knowledge and for the betterment of our society "A pen is a waepon which is 10x effective ,anyway what are the ninja techniques to study !

1. First of all know your potential if you can memorise one paragraph within 1 hour if not don't worry ,you are not inferior to others ,Do our five fingers in hand are saame ? No still they work as important as rest of the fingers . You will often hear people saying wake up early , you will be able to score good marks .These are all myths ,well there is a scientific reason behind it . The hours during morning passes slow in contrast to evening so we get more time to study .

2. Studying whole day . Absolutely wrong ,just like our body it can't do work whole day it needs brake to rest to store its metabolism strength . Exactly our brain also needs some brake to function properly.

SEVEN
EXAGGERATING

Often I have recognise one thing ,while you are scrolling any motivational videos ,each videos will suggest you some tips though the tips might not be same .Don't just simply apply them in your life , think about it wisely every person have different ways of syudying ,some tips are useful so don't be in rush apply them slowly in your life

Life becomes a long journey when we have to face sadness whereas it becomes short when we have to face happiness .

Enter Caption

EIGHT

MENTAL HEALTH & FAILURE

Almost every person in this world might have suffer failure atleast once in their life .Failure plays a crucial role in our life there is no satisfication in acheiving sucess without failure and hardwork . Don't be scared of failure ,failure makes us more poweful and a determined person.

Just like physical health our mental health is also important ,How can it be cured ? Simply by doing exercise ,meditation and consulting to a psychologists . There are many Mental Health issues like depression ,anxiety ,panic attack, Bipolar Disorder don't be afraid you are not the one who is suffering from it . There are many people who are suffering it and are seeking forward to cure it . Some of it are temporary while some remains permanent but can be cured with right treatment . Well some symptoms of anxiety are common in teenagers , these are temporary ,one more thing never feel scared or shy to ask your parents any questions which seems to be difficult for you to understand . What made all these issues created? well during lockdown all these issues were created ,all the things happened in online mode ,no interaction .But don't worry just like a black cloud cast shadow only for sometime , eventually the sun shows up and removes all sadness .

Enter Caption

NINE
MIND TRIGGER

Don't feel like studying ? If you also don't feel like studying congratulations ! you are close to the reality , your actual journey starts when you don't feel like studying because good things always take time to become a habit ,but once you gain it ,you will become the most satisfied person in your life .Now how to not get distracted by social media obviously following a schedule strictly is just not possible . First step we can do is just deleting social media or logging out of it, one of the best trick you can do is switching off your mobile , scrolling your phone is a simultaneous process even if you restart your phone it takes time to operate your phone .so your desire to scroll your mobile ends

How to start studying ?

Its pretty eassy . There are many people I have seen starting their studies from middle portion of their chapters .Start studying from the beginning ,no worry you can byheart the answer ,write it in your exam ,get good marks but if your concept is not clear you will feel emptiness in your life regretting your past decession .No matter even the problem is of the grade 3 ,clear it otherwise ,those doubts will become an obstacle for the sucess of your life .Now how many of you have dreamt of becoming a topper of your class,school and college .Everyone isn't .But few of you might have dreamt of becoming topper of your mind ,soul

TEN
WHO IS A TOPPER ?

Competiton is normal in today's generation ? But with how many people will you compete? At a time you can only beat few people of your class .Though there are some extraordinary people like Jeff Becoz ,Elon musk but they were not intended to be genius from childhood ,during their childhood they were similar to common children .But one thing this famous people have in their life is a strong mindset and willingness to learn something . Dream big ! Don't be afraid to dream but while dreaming keep one thing in your mind " Continue working with that don't exaggerate .We often feel that the topper is a genius ,he did not need to study a lot ,he easily remembers all the things that is one of our misconception .We often get motivated for a few time watching youtube videos but those are temporary ,youtube motivation can help you to understand the importance of studies or waste your time . Instead of watching that 5 mins motivational videos you could have done 3 or 4 sums . Utilise your time , your small efforts will create a bright outcome .Create your timetable in the beginning you might have less topics to cover don't just leave it saying ,these are too short ,I don't need such long ways to complete it but you will find that those topics will hamper your studies before exam ,start little but do complete ,suprisingly you will find you are improving daily ,then start increasing the difficulty level . At a time your brain will be properly trained and you will be able to acquire all the information .Have patience .

ELEVEN
TAKING RISK

Taking risks won't provide you a chance or upragadation . All the acheivements in your life depends on your efforts and perseverance
.

What I learn from my failure .

1. If you are not sure with your compatibility then don't take risk or else it make your work more worse then it were before .

2. Take risk according to your capacity , you won't gain without lossing.

3. Not everything happens for a reason some occurs to teach you a lesson .

4. Try to be satisfied with whatever you have never complain about your life . You and they are completely different .

5.Always try to be the best version of yourself .

TWELVE

LESSONS TO LEARN FROM FAILURE .

1. Patience is necessary .
2. Have a calm mind.
3. It shows your reflection.
4. It made me realise that truely not everyone has same level of IQ but each of us have some unique features.
5. Each child is precious .
6. Over confidence kills a person.
7. Try to be satisfied with the level of work that you are doing.
8. Keep working hard!Have patience ... Everyone's time comes

Miracle happens sometimes ....

Evolution! Of the reality ... Indeed ?? Glory! Culmination......

Advance Praise for *Staying Freelance*

"An intriguing exploration into an aspect of book publishing that is unfamiliar to most readers. Reider's spirited resolve to enter and maintain her career through its many ups and downs is both interesting and inspiring. I learned a lot about the subject and the author!"

—Fred Gottlieb, editor

"Most online freelancing gurus help beginners get in the game, but they don't tell you how to stay in it. Andrea is the real deal—in *Staying Freelance,* she writes honestly and unapologetically about how to win the freelancing game."

—Jessica Andersen, Brand Book consultant

"This book is a must-read for those who are considering becoming consultants in any field and for many who have already begun. As a professional consultant of many years, I wholeheartedly relate to and agree with Andrea's accounting of her experience and what it takes to maintain a successful continuing business."

—Martin Gantman, architect and consulting civil engineer

"Working with Andrea was simply a dream. She is one of those freelancers that is easy to work with (half the task) and knowledgeable. Her deep experience in the field was evident. Thank you for all your hard work!"

—Laurie Chow, senior graphic production artist

"Reider shares her journey from freelance typesetter to book designer, giving readers a firsthand account of her successes, failures, and thought processes during those times. *Staying Freelance* is a testament to perseverance and creativity and a must-read for freelancers."

—Robin Kellogg, author and book coach

"This book is inspiring. Andrea Reider describes the high-wire act of freelance book design and typesetting while keeping it real. In a business where radical change is the norm, she demonstrates how to negotiate success, failure, and everything in between. Reider's book is exemplary. It will inspire you even if you are in a different line of work or just living your life. Read it!"

—Cynthia A. Sowers, Senior Lecturer (Emerita),
Arts and Ideas in the Humanities,
The Residential College, The University of Michigan

"Andrea has proven herself to be multitalented in the typesetting world—pivoting easily between very different types of books. A freelancer before freelancing became well-known, she has so much wisdom to offer. Freelance to me equals freedom, and Andrea outlines what has worked for her in a clear, concise manner. A superb guide to breaking free from traditional office work to striking out on your own and loving the work you do!"

—Shelly Mateer, author

"I love this book so much as I'm a freelance writer and it took a lot of courage to become one. This book has the potential to inspire future freelancers so they too can experience the freedom of freelancing!"

—Corrine Casanova, founder of Corrine the Content Queen

"Through tenacity, grit, and a little luck, Andrea built a career that works for her, and her story shows the possibilities and freedoms freelancing provides while inspiring new freelancers to create their own storied careers."

—Fallon Clark, book developer and revision guide